123

Jesus Loves Me
for Little Ones

Rebecca Lutzer

Illustrated by Mary Eakin

HARVEST
kids

HARVEST HOUSE PUBLISHERS
EUGENE, OREGON

Unless otherwise indicated, all Scripture quotations are taken from The ESV® Bible (The Holy Bible, English Standard Version®), copyright © 2001 by Crossway, a publishing ministry of Good News Publishers. Used by permission. All rights reserved.

Verses marked NIV are taken from the Holy Bible, New International Version®, NIV®. Copyright © 1973, 1978, 1984, 2011 by Biblica, Inc.® Used by permission of Zondervan. All rights reserved worldwide. www.zondervan.com. The "NIV" and "New International Version" are trademarks registered in the United States Patent and Trademark Office by Biblica, Inc.®

For bulk, special sales, or ministry purchases, please call 1-800-547-8979.
Email: Customerservice@hhpbooks.com

Cover and interior design by Mary Eakin

This logo is a federally registered trademark of the Hawkins Children's LLC. Harvest House Publishers, Inc., is the exclusive licensee of this trademark.

123 Jesus Loves Me for Little Ones

Text copyright © 2023 by Rebecca Lutzer
Artwork copyright © 2023 by Mary Eakin
Published by Harvest House Publishers
Eugene, Oregon 97408
www.harvesthousepublishers.com

ISBN 978-0-7369-8785-1 (hardcover)

Library of Congress Control Number: 2023934344

Printed in China

23 24 25 26 27 28 29 30 31 / LP / 10 9 8 7 6 5 4 3 2 1

This book is dedicated to all the children who will hear or read its pages. Jesus said, "Let the little children come to me" (Matthew 19:14). He took the children in his arms and blessed them. YOU are very special to Jesus and he loves you.

One
1

One Star

Jesus the Savior was born in the town of Bethlehem. Wise men from a country far away wanted to find Jesus and worship him. God put **one** special star in the sky to guide them. It was a long journey and took many months for them to reach Bethlehem. The wise men watched the star and followed it until it stopped over the place where the child was. They went into the house and found Jesus with his mother, Mary, and knelt down and worshipped him. They gave him special gifts of gold, frankincense, and myrrh.

MATTHEW 2:1-2, 7-11

LESSON
I can worship Jesus the Savior who is Christ the Lord.

Two

Two Boats

Jesus loved to tell people about his Father who lived in heaven. He would teach from God's Word and tell stories to help them understand who he was. Many people followed him everywhere to listen to his words. He would teach in the temple, sitting on a hillside, or walking along a road. One day the people crowded around Jesus as he taught them on the seashore. He saw two boats at the water's edge left there by the fishermen who were washing their nets. He got into the boat that belonged to Simon, and it was pushed out into the water. Then Jesus sat down and taught the people from the boat.

LUKE 5:1-3

LESSON
I can listen to what Jesus taught because he is very wise.

Three

Three Days

When Jesus was twelve years old, he went with his parents, Mary and Joseph, to the city of Jerusalem to celebrate a special dinner called the feast of Passover. At the end of the feast, his parents and friends left to travel back home. But Jesus stayed in Jerusalem and did not go with them. When Mary and Joseph realized that Jesus wasn't with them, they returned to Jerusalem and searched for him for **three** days. They found him in the temple court, sitting among the teachers. He was listening to them and asking questions. Jesus told his parents that he needed to be in his Father's house.

LUKE 2:41-49

LESSON
As I grow up, I want to learn about God.

Four Friends

One day Jesus was teaching the people in the town of Capernaum. So many crowded into a house to listen to him that there was no more room. **Four** men brought their friend who couldn't walk to see Jesus. But the doorway was blocked by the crowd, and they couldn't get inside. So they lifted the mat with their friend onto the roof. They removed some roof tiles and lowered their friend into the middle of the crowd right in front of Jesus! When Jesus saw their faith, he said to the crippled man, "Son, your sins are forgiven. . . Get up, take your mat and go home." And that's exactly what he did! All the people praised God for this miracle.

MARK 2:1-12 (NIV)

LESSON
I can help my friends
learn about Jesus too.

Five
5

Five Loaves

Jesus went up on a mountainside to spend time with his close friends he called disciples. But a big crowd of people followed them. Jesus knew the people were hungry after walking so far. He asked his disciples where they could buy enough bread to feed all of them. One disciple saw a boy with his lunch of five barley loaves of bread and two small fish. The boy gave his lunch to Jesus, who took the loaves and fish and gave thanks. Jesus did a miracle by making the loaves and fish turn into many pieces. It was enough to feed all the people. There were so many pieces left over that they filled twelve baskets!

JOHN 6:3-13

LESSON
I can help others by sharing my things with them.

Six Jars

Jesus and his disciples were invited to a wedding. At the dinner there was food to eat and special grape juice called wine to drink. But there was not enough juice to serve everyone. Jesus's mother told him that the guests needed more wine. So Jesus asked the waiters to fill six very large jars with water, then draw some out to serve the guests. When it was served to the master of the wedding dinner, it was no longer water but tasted like the best wine. Jesus had done a miracle by turning the water into wine. This showed the people that he was the Son of God.

JOHN 2:1-11

LESSON
I can ask Jesus to help me when I have a problem.

Seven Miles

One day two men were walking from the city of Jerusalem to the town of Emmaus. It was a long walk of seven miles. As they walked and talked, a stranger began to walk with them. He asked them why they looked so sad. They explained that their friend Jesus had died and been buried in a grave. Then this man began to tell them many things about Jesus. When they reached the town, they sat down to eat dinner. The stranger took the bread and gave thanks to God for the food. Suddenly, the two men knew that this man was Jesus. He had risen from the grave and was alive! Then Jesus disappeared from their presence and they were alone. The men were so excited that they walked all the way back to Jerusalem to tell the disciples that Jesus was alive!

LUKE 24:13-35

LESSON
Even though I can't see Jesus,
I know he is with me every day.

Eight Days

Jesus's disciples were very sad when he died and were slow to believe that he was alive again. **Eight** days after he had risen from the grave, the disciples were meeting together in a house and the doors were locked. Suddenly, Jesus came and stood among them and said, "Peace be with you." To prove that it was really him, Jesus showed them the wounds in his hands and side. The disciples knew and believed that this truly was their friend Jesus, the Son of God.

JOHN 20:26-29

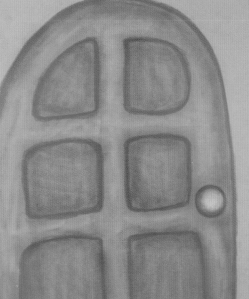

LESSON
I believe that Jesus is the Son of God, and that he died to forgive my sins.

Nine Lepers

Jesus was walking with his disciples when he met ten men who were sick with a skin disease called leprosy. They stood at a distance and called out loudly, "Jesus, Master, have mercy on us." Jesus cared about them, so he did a miracle. He healed their skin and made them clean. Nine of the men walked away without thanking Jesus. Only one man came back to say "thank you." And Jesus asked, "Where are the nine? They did not return and give praise to God. Only this one man who is from another country." So Jesus gave him a special blessing.

LUKE 17:11-19

LESSON
I will give thanks to Jesus for the blessings of my family, food, friends, and toys.

Ten

Ten Young Women

Jesus told a story about **ten** young women who were invited by a king to a wedding dinner. When they went out to meet him, they took their lamps with them. But they had to wait a long time for the king to arrive, and they fell asleep. Suddenly, they heard someone call out, "Here's the king! Come out to meet him!" Only five of the young women were wise and remembered to put extra oil in their lamps. They lit their lamps and were ready when the king arrived. He took them to the wedding dinner and then shut the door. The other five young women were foolish and did not have enough oil to light their lamps. They were not ready when the king arrived, and they missed the dinner.

MATTHEW 25:1-13

LESSON
I want to be ready to meet Jesus in heaven someday.

Dear Little One,

This is a special book. While you learn to count from 1 to 10, you will also learn about Jesus. He is your Savior, your friend, and your helper. Jesus loves YOU. He wants you to know and love him too. Have fun counting with Jesus!

From my heart to yours,

"Grandma Rebecca"